A magnificent giant-sized twin-cylindered horizontal Marklin electric-light plant with a working ball-weight governor, lever safety valve, cylinder lubricators and boiler platform, dating from about 1912.

TOY STEAM ENGINES

Bob Gordon

Shire Publications Ltd

CONTENTS

Copyright © 1985 by Bob Gordon. First published 1985. Shire Album 137. ISBN 0 85263 775 6.

Set in 9 point Times roman and printed in Great Britain by C. I. Thomas & Sons (Haverfordwest) Ltd, Press Buildings, Merlins Bridge, Haverfordwest, Dyfed.

British Library Cataloguing in Publication data available.

ACKNOWLEDGEMENTS
The author is indebted to W. E. Finlayson, Basil Harley and Jack Mercer for reading and commenting on the manuscript, to Peter Mole for photographic work and to Ann Speedy for line drawings. He is also grateful for the helpful co-operation received from New Cavendish Books, the Justin Knowles Publishing Group, Jonathan Minns of the British Engineerium, Allen Levy of the London Toy and Model Museum, D. R. Beasley of New York, P. M. Sears of Washington DC, W. H. Gottschalk of Paxton, Carlernst A. Baecker of Frankfurt, Bassett-Lowke (Railways) Limited, the staff of Steam Age, Mamod Limited, Wilhelm Schroder and Company, and the Jensen Manufacturing Company Incorporated. Illustrations on the following pages are reproduced by kind permission of: Bassett-Lowke (Railways) Limited, Steam Age, 10 (upper left), 22 (upper); British Engineerium, 15 (lower); Cecil Collection, 7 (right), 8, 9, 16 (left), 17, 20 (right), 22 (lower); Dibbler Collection, 6, 12, 15 (upper right), 16 (right), 19 (upper and lower right), 20 (left), 23 (upper), 24 (right), front cover; A. W. Gamage, 25 (lower), 27 (lower); William H. Gottschalk, 23 (lower); Basil Harley collection, 4, 13 (lower), 14, 15 (upper left), 26; Jensen Manufacturing Company Incorporated, 31 (lower right); Justin Knowles Publishing Group, 7 (left), 10 (lower); London Toy and Model Museum, 25 (upper); Malins (Engineering) Limited, 11; Mamod Limited, 31 (upper); Model and Allied Publications Limited, 5; Museum of London, 24 (left); New Cavendish Books, 3, 10 (upper right); Wilhelm Shroder and Company, 31 (lower left); Smithsonian Institution, photo number 79-6508, 13 (upper); photo number 79-6506, 19 (lower left), photo number 79-6507, 21; Stuart Turner, 2; Geoff Wright and Roy Hallsworth, 30. The picture on page 27 (upper) is reproduced from Die Anderen Nürnberger.

COVER: A fine Doll horizontal piston-valve electric-light plant with lighting column and open-coil 1.5 volt dynamo. The engine has a piston-rod guide rail and an eccentric-operated feed pump and was made about 1925.

LEFT: A Frisbie horizontal overtype engine made by J. and E. Stevens and Company, Connecticut, of about 1871. It had a cast iron boiler and patent valve gear operated from the connecting rod without the use of an eccentric.

The factory of Georges Carette and Company, Nuremberg, manufacturers of mechanical, optical, electrical and physical toys and working models.

INTRODUCTION

There is a special fascination about toy steam engines seldom found with other mechanical toys, and they have a timeless appeal far beyond that of being just children's playthings. Not only do they work without being wound up, but they are noisy, smelly and often dirty as well, just like the real thing. And above all they project an image of boisterous power.

In Great Britain, a country which did so much to promote steam power, it is not surprising that miniature engines of the stationary type, operated by live steam, became one of the most popular toys for boys during the late Victorian and Edwardian periods. These periods were notable for the excellence of the steam toys produced, toys which were among the finest examples of the toymaker's art and which now mirror for us the past splendour of the massive steam engines which powered the industrial revolution.

The types of stationary engine used in industry during the nineteenth century were many and varied and toymakers had a wide range of prototypes to choose from. The variety of toy engines manufactured was amazing and many of the illustrations in this book give an indication of their charm. They will also revive happy and nostalgic memories of a bygone age in which steam was king.

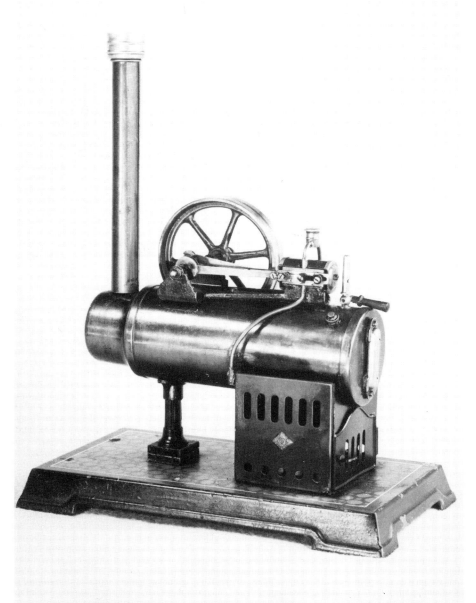

A Bing semi-portable overtype engine with external slide-valve arrangement, boiler-barrel support column and locomotive-type firebox. About 1912.

4

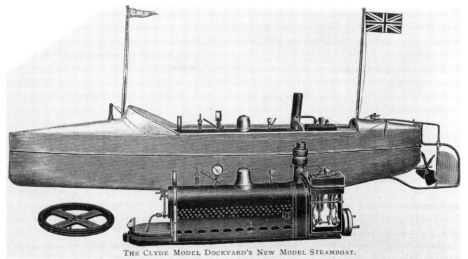

THE CLYDE MODEL DOCKYARD'S NEW MODEL STEAMBOAT.

A twin-cylindered dual-purpose marine plant made by the Clyde Model Dockyard about 1920. It could be converted for stationary use by attaching a larger flywheel to the solid one and so drive accessories.

TOY STEAM ENGINES

The first miniature steam engine was made by Hero, a Greek mathematician, in the first century AD. This was his sphere of Aeolus, for which steam power was used to rotate a metal ball mounted on pivots. Models of this ancient steam toy were being sold in the streets of London in 1888 for one old penny.

The first practical steam machine, a full-sized atmospheric beam engine made by Thomas Newcomen, was installed in a colliery in Staffordshire in 1712. This historic event was followed by the introduction of many different kinds of stationary steam engine, and these were soon being reproduced in miniature as playthings for boys.

A number of firms in Britain, Europe and the United States started making steam engines, and the most prominent toymakers were the Germans, who pioneered the mass-production of cheap and attractive steam toys.

The German engines were visually exciting and huge quantities were exported to Britain and the United States. The designs were imaginative, there was a vast array to choose from and, above

all, the Germans gave a lot of care and attention to detail to make their toys resemble real engines. If the prototype steam plant had a brick chimney stack, then the toy version usually had simulated brickwork as well, not just a piece of brass tubing like some of the British and American ones.

Although many of the German steam engines were never intended to be accurate replicas, their special appeal was that they encapsulated the period charm of the originals and gave a working illusion of the real thing. The Germans were experts at making toy engines that were a fascinating mixture of truth and make-believe and which were representative of steam engines generally without necessarily being based upon specific prototypes.

Many of the German engines were painted in bright colours. They often had baseplates with simulated tiling and the more expensive ones simply bristled with steam whistles, gauges, steam domes, safety valves, ball-weight governors, handrails, walkways and ladders. Miniature manometers or steam gauges were also fitted, but these were more for show than for serious use. The fittings were usually nickel-plated, and the engines were sometimes given names such as *Ideal, Marvel* or *Vulcan* and were so pleasing to the eye that children loved them.

An amazing variety of toy steam engines was made, ranging from simple impulse turbines to the most magnificent power stations. One of the cheapest steam engines ever marketed by the German toymakers was a Carette steam turbine. Illustrated in the 1911 catalogue, this consisted of a simple paddle-wheel type rotor mounted on top of a plain vertical boiler and driven by a jet of steam impinging on the rotor blades.

In constrast to this was a superb Marklin electric-light plant in which the chimney stack was almost 48 inches high (1220 mm). The baseplate, measuring 33½ by 35 inches (850 by 890 mm), was made in two sections which clipped together. On one side was a horizontal boiler 9 inches in diameter by 23 inches long (230 by 580 mm), of the semi-internally fired type with cross tubes. On the other side a large twin-cylinder horizontal engine, mounted on a cast iron plinth, drove an electrical generator by means of a belt from the rim of the flywheel. This magnificent steam plant, only a few of which were made, was probably the largest ever to appear in a toy catalogue.

In between these two extremes was a vast miscellany of fascinating steam engines and they were of six main types: beam, horizontal, vertical, overtype, marine and portable engines. There were many variants such as bottle-frame, duplex and triplex, compound, uniflow, donkey, crane and fire engines, turbines and special steam plants.

A rare and interesting Marklin portable engine, made about 1919, which could be converted to a semi-portable or a vertical stationary engine. Called a 'dual purpose convertible', this steam toy was fitted with a spark arrester on the chimney.

6

LEFT: *A duplex engine with twin boilers and twin-cylindered engine on a simulated tiled base. Made by Ernst Plank, this engine was sold by Gamages in 1906 for one guinea.*
RIGHT: *A Falk semi-portable overtype engine of about 1920, complete with heavy flywheel, walkway platforms, feed pump and spark arrester on the chimney.*

HOW TOY STEAM ENGINES WORK

Water contains locked-up energy and a steam engine is a machine for releasing this energy, by the application of heat, and converting it into mechanical energy.

Water which is heated in an open container boils at 212 Fahrenheit (100 Celsius) but does not produce any useful steam pressure; it merely counterbalances the atmospheric pressure of 14.71 pounds per square inch (1.03 kg/sq cm), which is marked as 0 pounds per square inch (psi), on a steam pressure gauge. However, if water is heated in an enclosed boiler the steam pressure can be raised by applying heat in excess of the normal boiling point of 212 Fahrenheit. This is because the steam, being unable to escape to the atmosphere, exerts pressure on the surface of the water below it, retards the formation of steam bubbles and becomes compressed into a smaller space. The more it is compressed the higher will be its pressure and more and more heat will be needed to create steam. It was this pressure additional to

that of the atmosphere that was used to drive steam engines, and to prevent dangerous pressures building up inside boilers spring or lever type safety valves were fitted so that excess steam could be released.

When the steam cocks on toy boilers were opened the steam expanded and flowed under pressure to the engines and moved the pistons to and fro inside the cylinders. Even after the steam was cut off by the steam valves it continued to expand and exert force.

Cylinders were of two kinds, oscillating and fixed. Oscillating cylinders were usually single-action types in which the steam was admitted and exhausted by the pivotal movement of the cylinders across the steam ports in the steam distribution blocks. As the cylinders swivelled, the motion of the pistons was conveyed directly to the crankshafts by the piston rods, causing them to turn.

In the case of fixed cylinders, these were usually double-action types in which the steam was admitted alternately at the backs and fronts of the pistons, the steam inlet and exhaust ports being controlled by valves operated from eccentric sheaves on the crankshafts. The amount by which the eccentrics were 'out of centre' was designed to give the desired travel to the valves. The valves in toy engines were usually slide valves working inside steam chests, but sometimes the valves were held in position by balls and springs fixed on the outside of the cylinders. Piston valves were fitted to some engines, and others had poppet valves operated by camshafts turned by bevel gears from the crankshafts.

As the pistons in fixed cylinders did not swivel, pivoted connecting rods were attached to the piston rods so that the motion could be conveyed to the crankshafts. As steam exerted pressure on the pistons in a series of thrusts, single or twin flywheels were always attached to the crankshafts. These acted as reservoirs of kinetic energy and provided momentum to smooth out any jerkiness of the motion and prevent speed fluctuations. On some toy engines working speed

A fine Marklin horizontal, double expansion simulated compound engine on a cast iron plinth and metal baseplate and complete with feed pump, steam dome, lever safety valve and four cup lubricators. About 1913.

LEFT: *A rare Doll horizontal 'valve machine' or uniflow-type engine with special vertical-acting piston valves operated by eccentrics on a shaft driven by bevel gearing from the crankshaft. About 1930.*

RIGHT: *A Marklin donkey engine with a domed-top copper boiler, inclined fixed-cylinder engine with overhung disc crank and split eccentric reversing. About 1905.*

governors were also fitted, but for the most part these ball-weight governors were for show only and did not control the engine speed.

Some engines were provided with mechanisms which reversed the direction of rotation. This was achieved by moving plates with levers attached, which changed the relative positions of the steam and exhaust ports. Another method of reversing was by means of slip eccentrics, which were set by the adjustment of two stops on the shafts.

OPERATION AND MAINTENANCE

As some of the early engines are now antiques, collectors are concerned about keeping them in good condition, and many prized engines are never steamed. Nevertheless, a surprising number of engines made around 1900 are still in working order and half the fun of ownership is to see them in motion. Although toy-type boilers usually work at very low pressures of between 10 and 25 psi, (0.70 to 1.76 kg/sq cm), it is advisable to have them examined by a competent person before raising steam to ensure that they are safe to use and that the safety valve is set correctly and is in working order.

Collector's items should always be kept in a clean condition, and if engines are used they should be cleaned and oiled and the boilers emptied and dried out after use.

Great care should be taken not to damage the original paintwork, which should be cleaned with a soft cloth moistened with a mixture of paraffin and lubricating oil. Abrasive powders should never be used for cleaning, neither should friction be applied to any kind of painted trademark.

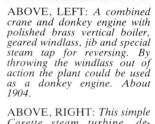

ABOVE, LEFT: *A combined crane and donkey engine with polished brass vertical boiler, geared windlass, jib and special steam tap for reversing. By throwing the windlass out of action the plant could be used as a donkey engine. About 1904.*

ABOVE, RIGHT: *This simple Carette steam turbine, described as the 'cheapest miniature steam engine', was priced at six shillings per dozen in 1911, or sixpence each.*

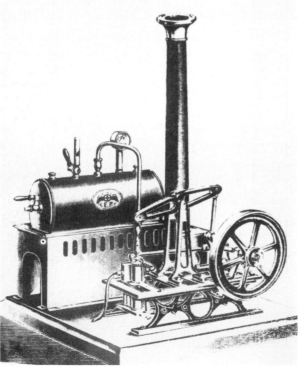

LEFT: *A 'Watt' single-cylinder two-pillar beam engine made by Ernst Plank. This was being sold by Gamages in 1902 for 35 shillings.*

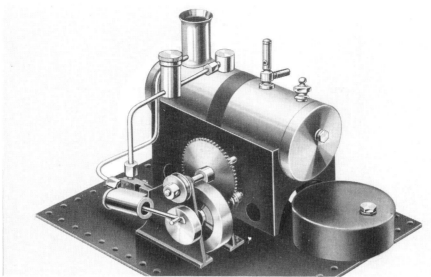

An early Hobbies SE3 horizontal engine, with locomotive-type chimney and solid brass flywheel, made by Malins for Hobbies Ltd about 1937. The reduced gear shaft and baseplate were designed for use with Meccano.

TYPES OF TOY STEAM ENGINE

BEAM ENGINES

A rotative two-pillar beam engine made of brass was shown in the Ernst Plank catalogue for 1902. Described as the 'Watt' beam engine, this had a horizontal boiler and was built on the Watt system. In this engine a vertical upward-thrusting piston tilted one end of a centrally pivoted beam and moved it up and down. This caused the crankshaft and flywheel (to which the other end of the beam was connected) to rotate. Relatively few of these German beam engines were made and they are a rare find today.

HORIZONTAL ENGINES

Horizontal steam plants had the engines, but not necessarily the boilers, mounted horizontally. In their simplest form the British ones consisted of 'waggle' type oscillating cylinders attached to the sides of tinplate fireboxes above which small 'pot' boilers, with wick-type spirit heaters, were mounted. Crankshafts were of the through-firebox types.

Lead flywheels, and sometimes spring safety valves and small chimneys, were provided. The German engines were usually mounted separately on the baseplates adjacent to the boilers, which were almost always provided with a chimney stack.

The more expensive toys, sometimes twin-cylindered with twin or triple boilered mill engines, had either oscillating or fixed-type cylinders. Brass or iron flywheels were fitted, together with lever safety valves, steam and water gauges and feed pumps. Organ-pipe or bell steam whistles were also provided, although they were apt to be disappointing as they tended to wheeze and splutter rather than whistle.

Improved boilers were fitted with lacquered or oxidised finishes in blue or grey shades instead of polished brass. These were often heated by vaporising spirit heaters with multiple 'pepper pot' burners in which the vapour was produced by small pilot flames below them. Sometimes steam pipes were taken through the fireboxes on their way to the engines to dry out the steam, thus providing a crude form of superheating.

Cylinders on engines were not always what they seemed to be. A British-made Bowman engine, for example, had cylinders which looked like fixed ones but were actually oscillators working inside fixed brass cylinder casings.

VERTICAL ENGINES

Toy engines with upright cylinders were called verticals, but marine types with downward-thrusting pistons were sometimes described, like their proto-

A compact horizontal mill engine and boiler on a cast iron base, made by Marklin about 1919. The double-action slide-valve engine has a lubricator cup and is fitted with piston rod and crank guards. The water-gauge glass has been removed.

types, as 'inverted' verticals. Also vertical engines with upward-thrusting pistons, and with the crankshafts and flywheels mounted overhead on centre pillars, were occasionally described as 'trestle support' engines.

Usually, but not always, the boilers for vertical engines were mounted vertically. Catalogue descriptions were not always a true guide to engine types because sometimes engines with horizontal boilers and vertical engines were described as being horizontal.

Simple vertical oscillators had brass boilers with through-boiler crankshafts, lead flywheels, safety valves, small chimneys and little else. On some of the cheap engines safety valves were omitted. The reason for this was that oscillating cylinders were held to the steam distribution blocks by springs. Consequently any excess of steam pressure forced the cylinders off and allowed the steam to escape. The safest arrangement was a combination of oscillators and safety valves.

For engines of all types with fixed cylinders safety valves were obligatory, and the more advanced vertical engines with centre-flue boilers had a full range of other fittings, including water gauges. On a Bing engine of about 1895 an unusual mechanical water indicator was fitted instead of the usual gauge glass. This consisted of a clock-type dial attached to the boiler, over which a pointer, operated by a float, moved to indicate the water level.

A vertical boiler illustrated in Gamages 1913 catalogue was provided with a novel method of water replenishment. Although described as an 'automatic injector', it appears to have been a water-circulating device rather than a steam injector.

Some of the superior German engines were described as being 'technically perfect' and were robustly made with burnished brass boilers, precision-built crankshafts, iron flywheels, water feed pumps, furnace doors, lubricating cups, steam cocks, heavy japanned cast iron bases and condensing tanks.

OVERTYPE ENGINES

Vertical overtype engines were made but the horizontal types mounted above

ABOVE: *A Weeden horizontal engine and boiler on cast iron base, with imitation ball-weight governor, of about 1920.*

RIGHT: *A well used Fleischmann horizontal engine of about 1930, with oscillating cylinder, overhung crank and simulated brickwork chimney.*

A through-boiler crank vertical engine of unknown make with solid flywheel and Bing accessory, made about 1910.

horizontal boilers were more popular. Some of the earliest and most unusual overtype engines were made in the United States. One, patented by Russell Frisbie, had a kettle-shaped cast iron boiler, on top of which a fixed-cylinder horizontal engine with special oscillating valve gear was mounted. The boiler had no firebox or chimney but was elevated on three legs, leaving room for an alcohol heater to be placed underneath. Only two kinds of Frisbie engine were marketed (the other was an overhead walking beam engine patented in 1871) and they are now very rare.

The German overtype engines usually had horizontal boilers mounted on conventional or locomotive-type fireboxes, and they were fitted with chimneys.

MARINE ENGINES

Because of the need to conserve space, inverted vertical engines with the cylinder heads uppermost and with downward-thrusting pistons were developed for marine use. The toy engines mostly had horizontal boilers and were equipped with small but solidly made disc-type brass flywheels, to which the propeller shafts were coupled. Typical examples were the ST plants introduced by Stuart Turner in the 1920s. These had single-cylinder vertical engines and horizontal boilers enclosed in metal casings with polished copper funnels on top.

PORTABLE ENGINES

Portable engines were mounted on wheels so they could be moved about, often by horses. Most toy portables could be self-propelled by attaching a chain to the flywheel and one of the driving wheels. They usually had locomotive type boilers and high smoke stacks, with spark arresters on top, which could be lowered when travelling, and an overtype engine with horizontal cylinders. Perforated metal flame guards were often fitted to prevent the spirit heaters from being blown out.

ABOVE, LEFT: *A Schoenner vertical engine and boiler of about 1905, with an unusual cast lead cylinder and overhung crank. A safety valve is not fitted.*

ABOVE, RIGHT: *A powerful Bing double-action vertical engine standing 21 inches (533 mm) high, made about 1912. The vertical centre-flue boiler, chimney and firebox are made of brass and the base and firedoor of cast iron.*

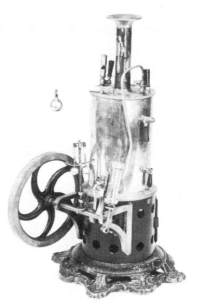

RIGHT: *A rare vertical engine with oscillating cylinder and curved-spoke flywheel, lever-type safety valve and imitation ball-weight governor. Believed to be by Bing and made about 1905.*

LEFT: *A fine robustly built vertical Falk engine of about 1912 with fixed cylinder, reversing wheel and geared feed pump.*

RIGHT: *'Hercules', a vertical centre-pillar trestle-type engine with oscillating cylinder, overhung crank, inset vertical boiler and lever-type spring-reset safety whistle. Made by Ernst Plank and believed to date from about 1900.*

Semi-portable engines without wheels, and with boiler-barrel supports at the front, were also made.

BOTTLE-FRAME ENGINES

'Bottle' was the name sometimes used to describe marine-type vertical engines mounted on vee-shaped frames. Usually fed from vertical boilers, engines of this sort, with the cylinder heads uppermost, tended to be bottle-shaped.

DUPLEX AND TRIPLEX ENGINES

Duplex plants usually had twin boilers and sometimes twin engines as well. An unusual plant of this kind, made by Ernst Plank, was equipped with two separate fireboxes and boilers and two oscillating cylinders mounted in opposition to operate a central flywheel. About 1919 Marklin made a rare triple-boilered electric-light plant with twin chimneys and a single-cylindered horizontal engine.

COMPOUND ENGINES

After leaving a cylinder, steam under pressure was still capable of further work, and in prototype engines it was used up to four times before being exhausted. A similar principle was used in some of the more elaborate steam toys, which were simulated double-expansion compound engines.

UNIFLOW ENGINES

Uniflow engines were usually single-cylinder horizontal types in which steam was admitted by special vertically acting drop-type inlet valves at each end of the cylinder in turn. The steam was then exhausted from ports in the centre of the cylinder, which were uncovered by the piston itself. Comparatively few uniflow

engines of the toy variety were made and they are now hard to find.

DONKEY ENGINES

Donkey engines had vertical centre-flue boilers of brass or copper, often with domed tops and small chimneys. The boilers were usually mounted on cast iron bases, which also supported an inclined cylinder and flywheel. Reversing gear was usually provided.

CRANE ENGINES

Crane engines were similar to donkey

A Bing steam plant of about 1902 with the name 'Vanna' on the imitation brickwork chimney. The twin-cylindered vertical marine-type engine is not original although it is believed to be by Bing. The plant was originally fitted with a single-cylinder horizontal slide-valve engine.

17

engines but were mounted on revolving platforms attached to undercarriages fitted with wheels for running on toy railway lines. Crane girder jibs were provided and there were usually throw-off levers as well to disengage the cranes and convert them into donkey engines.

FIRE ENGINES

The first steam fire engines were horse-drawn and steam power was used for pumping only. The toy fire engines usually had polished brass boilers and powerful pumping engines mounted vertically at the back of horse-drawn carriages.

More ornate American-type steam pumpers were also made by the American and German toymakers and some of these fire engines were steam-driven.

TURBINES

Turbines were non-reciprocating steam engines. These toys were simpler than reciprocating engines because they did not work by steam *pressure,* but depended for their operation upon the *velocity* of steam issuing from nozzles and turning rotor blades. With speeds up to ten thousand revolutions per minute, they ran much faster than other toy engines, and reduction gearing was fitted to enable accessories to be driven.

SPECIAL STEAM PLANTS

Many special steam plants were made. These ranged from simple engine sheds with open sides and just a tin roof to large and elaborate lithographed engine halls with separate boiler and engine rooms. The boilers were often enclosed in imitation brickwork furnaces, and the engine rooms were decorated with simulated tilework floors and walls. To make them even more realistic, steam from the mill engines was exhausted up the chimney stacks, some of which were fitted with lightning conductors. This did not always satisfy the young engine drivers, who preferred real smoke. Occasionally they provided it themselves by filling the spirit heaters with bicycle-lamp oil, much to the detriment of the playroom ceilings.

Other special steam plants included complete breweries, butter manufactories and electric-light plants. Every steam-orientated schoolboy longed to own a miniature power station in which the engine drove a dynamo or alternator. Lighting columns were often provided and sometimes switchboards as well. These plants really generated electricity — not a lot, but just enough to light a few lamps in a dolls' house. A good head of steam was necessary, and when the lights were switched on the engines tended to slow down or stop as a result of the extra load thrown upon them.

Electric-light plants were brought up to date in 1958 when a 'Wilesco' atomic power station was introduced, complete with simulated reactor cupola and cooling tower. However, this innovative steam plant never became popular and soon went out of production.

ACCESSORIES

One of the exciting things about the early steam engines was the wide variety of accessories that were made to be driven by them. These novel and brightly coloured toys ranged from circular saws to complete factory workshops. An infinite variety of models with moving tinplate figures was also produced, together with windmills, dredgers, waterwheels and multi-jet fountains. They were all working toys and some of the most fascinating were the optical zoetropes, which gave an 'exhibition of living pictures', and the fairground swingboats with their musical-box accompaniments. Some accessories were also made with inbuilt power units and rotated by jets of steam or by reciprocating engines.

In 1902 Frank Hornby, an Englishman, introduced a constructional toy called 'Mechanics Made Easy'. This became known as 'Meccano' and boys who owned Meccano sets were able to construct their own accessories. Two Meccano steam engines were introduced by Meccano Ltd. The first, probably German, came out in about 1914 but did not last long, and another, of Meccano's own make was brought out in 1929. After 1935 production apparently ceased until 1965, when a new engine was made for Meccano by Malins (Engineering) Ltd.

HEATERS

In the vintage days of steam toys nearly all the engines were fired by methylated

RIGHT: *A rare overtype engine with oscillating cylinder and combined vertical boiler and fretted firebox made of brass. Make unknown but possibly American and made about 1880.*

BELOW, LEFT: *A Weeden vertical engine and boiler with oscillating cylinder and through-boiler crankshaft of about 1920.*

BELOW, RIGHT: *A Bing overtype oscillating cylinder engine with overhung crank, and with the maker's trademark embossed on the end drum of the boiler. Made about 1905.*

19

LEFT: *A fixed-cylinder overtype engine with bent crank, heavy flywheel and gear drive to the feed pump. The ladders to the walkways and the chimney are not original. Believed to be by Schoenner and made about 1910.*

RIGHT: *A Doll overtype twin-cylindered engine with twin flywheels, lever safety valve, imitation ball-weight governor, ladders and walkways. It has a double-burner vaporising spirit heater and the firebox, made from a set of heavy castings, has five vent holes on each side. Made about 1925.*

spirits, known in the United States as medical or wood alcohol. Some heaters were badly designed and had a nasty habit of catching fire and enveloping the whole plant in flames, with disastrous results to the paintwork. These conflagrations added to the excitement of engine driving and mischievous boys have been known to overfill the spirit heaters deliberately to cause spectacular flare-ups. However, playing with steam engines became less hazardous when solid-fuel spirit tablets became available in the 1940s for use instead of liquid fuel. These tablets have since become mandatory for use with steam toys.

The first spirit heaters were single-wick types but as the size of boilers increased various kinds of multiple burners were provided, including vaporising types which produced jets of hot blue flames. Heaters were usually designed so that the fuel would be exhausted before the water got too low in the boilers. In the 1920s some European and American manufacturers also fitted their boilers with electric heaters operated from the mains supply. It is hoped that all those early electrically heated boilers had overtemperature protection of the type now required.

A few American engines had no heaters at all and the boilers were designed to sit, like a kettle, over the fire in a kitchen stove.

An 'Empire' horizontal overtype engine with electrically heated boiler on a cast iron base. Made by the Metalware Corporation, Two Rivers, Wisconsin, it is believed to date from about 1940.

MANUFACTURERS AND RETAILERS

BRITISH MANUFACTURERS

Probably the first British firm to sell steam toys was John Bateman and Company (founded 1774). Others were the Clyde Model Dockyard (1789), Stevens's Model Dockyard (1843), Whitneys (1877), Bonds (1887), Bassett-Lowke (1899) and Stuart Turner (1906).

The early British steam engines were robustly built, mainly of brass or cast iron, and were often based on actual prototypes. At first they were hand-made for the sons of the rich and were usually adult toys or models rather than playthings for children.

Although Bassett-Lowke built up his reputation by making what he described as 'perfectly made, exquisitely finished, scientifically designed masterpieces in miniature', he also sold some German tinplate-type steam engines. Stuart Turner made toy marine engines but he also specialised, and the firm still does, in making precision-built scale model steam engines.

Following the outbreak of the First World War the export of toys from Germany ceased and a number of other British firms then started making steam engines. Among them were W. H. Jubb, Limited (founded 1915), Lewis Wild and Company (1916), Simpson Fawcett and Company (1919), Bar-Knight Model Engineering Company Limited (1920), Walter Piggot and Company (1920), F. Yates and Son Limited (1920s), Bowman Models (1923), Malins (Engineers) Limited (1936) and others. Malins initially made engines for Hobbies Limited, but started making their own 'Mamod' engines in 1937, and in 1985 Mamod Limited was acquired by Jedmond Engineers Limited and trades at Slough.

GERMAN MANUFACTURERS

Some of the German toymakers produced solidly built replica-type steam toys but the majority of their engines were not so robust or true to scale as the British ones, and a lot of tinplate was

ABOVE: *This horse-drawn fire engine was designed by Bassett-Lowke and made by Bing about 1902. With its solid brass flywheel, powerful pump, air chamber and two deliveries, this splendid steam toy was originally sold for 47s 6d.*
BELOW: *A fine horse-drawn steam fire pumper with a horizontal gear-driven pumping engine, air chamber and vertical boiler. Made by Marklin about 1913.*

RIGHT: *A horizontal poppet-valve electric-light plant with a water-storage tank around the chimney. Exhaust steam warmed the water which supplied the feed pump. The poppet valves were operated by eccentrics on a shaft turned by bevel gearing. Made by Bing about 1913.*

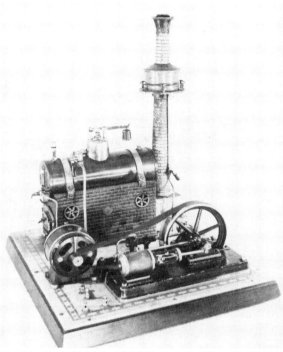

BELOW: *This steam fire pumper was one of Weeden's finest toys and had a twin oscillating-cylinder engine to drive the pump. Patented 1885.*

LEFT: *This ingenious toy was operated by a small steam turbine which caused the figure to dance. Manufactured by R. F. Benham of London about 1870, it was sold for 2s 6d.*
RIGHT: *An elegant Bing steam turbine of about 1900 with lever safety valve, steam and water gauges, bell whistle and an eight-wick spirit heater. The turbine rotor was designed to run at about eight thousand revolutions per minute. Reduction gearing reduced the speed of the driving pulley.*

used in their construction. Excellent steam engines were also made in France by the Paris firm of Radiguet (1872).

Most early tinplate-type steam engines were made in Nuremberg and among the foremost German toymakers were:

Bing Brothers, Nuremberg. By 1908 this firm, which was founded in 1863 by the brothers Adolph and Ignaz Bing, was claiming to be the 'greatest toy factory in the world'. In 1918 Stephan Bing took over the firm as Bing-Werke AG (Bing Limited). Because of financial problems the production of toys ceased about fourteen years later.

Carette, Nuremberg. Georges Carette, a Frenchman, started this business in 1886.

He traded as George Carette and Company and was associated for a time with both Bing and Bassett-Lowke. Business ceased in 1917.

Doll, Nuremberg. Peter Doll and J. Sondheim founded Doll and Company in 1898 to make steam engines and accessories. The firm was taken over by Fleischmann in the late 1930s.

Falk, Nuremberg. Joseph Falk left Carette's employment and started his own business about 1897. He specialised in steam engines, accessories and magic lanterns, and in 1910 he took over part of Jean Schoenner's toy business. In 1935 Falk was taken over by the successors of Ernst Plank.

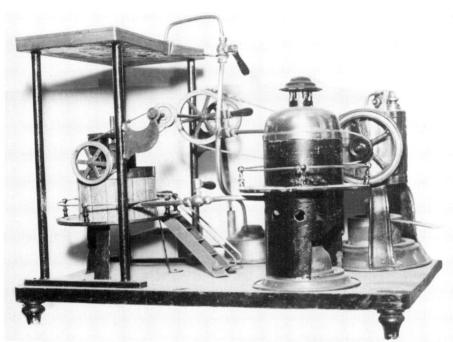

ABOVE: *A complete steam-driven brewery works including a brewing pan with heater, mash vat and circulating pump. Made by Ernst Plank about 1900.*

RIGHT: *A handsome engine hall with horizontal boiler and furnace enclosed in imitation masonry. The twin-cylindered horizontal slide-valve engine has a central flywheel driving line shafting on the wall in the tiled engine room. It was sold by Gamages in 1902 for 75 shillings.*

Maschinen-Halle

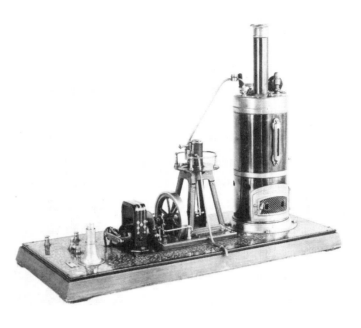

Fleischmann, Nuremberg. Jean Fleischmann founded Fleischmann Brothers in 1887 and managed the business until his death in 1917. His wife and brother then carried on and in 1938 the firm of Doll and Company was acquired. Fleischmann's two sons took control in 1940 and the firm is still in business.

Marklin, Goppingen. Theodore Marklin, maker of prestigious steam toys and doyen of the German toymakers, founded a business in 1859 which became one of the world's major suppliers of good-quality mechanical toys. After his death in 1866 his wife tried to keep the business going, but it was not until 1888, when her sons, Eugen, Karl and Wilhelm, joined the firm, that it prospered again. Trading was then carried out as Marklin Brothers until 1891, when a partner was taken on and the name was changed again to Marklin Brothers and Company. In 1922 it became a limited company. In the 1940s the manufacture of steam toys ceased but other toys are still made.

Ernst Plank, Nuremberg. Ernst Plank started making steam engines and magic

lanterns in 1866. Lack of finance led to a take-over by Fritz and Hans Schaler in 1930, and a few years later they took over the business of Falk as well.

J. Schoenner, Nuremberg. Founded in 1875, this firm made steam engines and other toys. It eventually closed down about 1910, when part of its production was taken over by Falk.

Wilhelm Schroder and Company, Ludenschied. Founded in 1912, this company made household goods and toys. It is still in business and its products include Wilesco steam engines, which continue the old German tradition for realistic steam toys of attractive appearance.

There were also many small German firms that made steam engines and marked them 'Made in Germany'.

AMERICAN MANUFACTURERS

Although many steam toys from Europe were exported to the United States, American firms also manufactured toy steam engines. These included J. and E. Stevens and Company (founded

26

RIGHT: *A fine precision built double action slide-valve steam engine with hand-operated feed pump, vaporising spirit heater, simulated brickwork boiler casing and protective fencing. Made by Ernst Plank about 1914.*

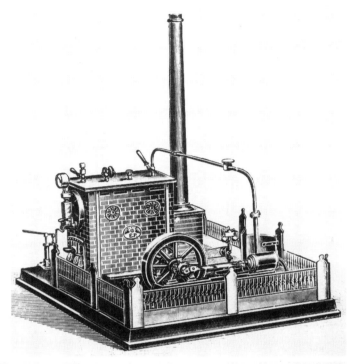

BELOW: *A selection of accessories for use with steam engines, sold by Gamages about 1900.*

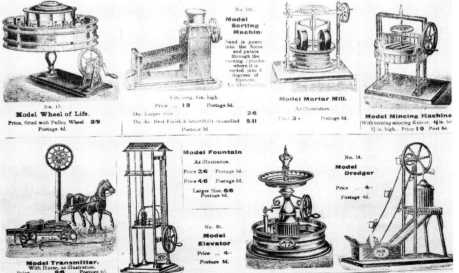

27

1843), manufacturers of cast iron hardware and toys, who made engines for Russell Frisbie (1871); Kraft and Huffington (1860s), taken over in 1869 by Alexander and Edward Buckman, who then set up the Buckman Manufacturing Company, which became noted for its 'Young America' steam engines; the Union Manufacturing Company (1870s), which later took over Buckman; Weeden Manufacturing Company (1877); Metal Ware Corporation (1920s), makers of 'Empire' steam engines; Jensen Manufacturing Company (1932); and the Major Toy Company Incorporated (1940s).

RETAILERS

By far the most popular British retailer of steam toys in the early days was Arthur Walter Gamage. He founded the famous Gamages store in Holborn in 1876, was an outstandingly innovative toy enthusiast, and his Grand Christmas Bazaar was the delight of every child fortunate enough to visit it. Gamage had a close relationship with the German toymakers and was able to purchase in bulk at special cheap rates. By 1906 he was offering vertical steam engines with simulated brickwork fireboxes and twin-wick spirit heaters for only 10½ old pence.

In the United States a firm that was set up specifically to sell steam toys for J. and E. Stevens and Company and George W. Brown and Company between 1868 and 1872 was the American Toy Company of New York. Montgomery Ward's large mail-order store, founded in 1872, was selling some steam engines in 1885. Another famous mail-order firm, Sears Roebuck and Company, was also selling Weeden steam engines around 1900.

28

IDENTIFICATION AND DATING

Many of the toy and model manufacturers, as well as the wholesalers and retailers, issued splendid catalogues, which were, and still are, of great assistance in establishing identity and date of manufacture. Patent Office registers are also valuable sources of information.

Problems of indentification often arise because some engines were sold without trade markings, and others were made by one toymaker for another. However, as there were sometimes slight variations between manufacturers in the designs used for steam whistles, steam cocks and governors, these variations became helpful in establishing identity. Dating of engines is often more difficult since certain designs were manufactured for long periods without alteration.

Almost everything Gamages sold could be ordered by post and the store's huge mail-order catalogue published in 1911 contained nine hundred pages. Other catalogues containing useful information about early steam engines are those issued by Christies, Sothebys and Phillips. Auctioneers' information is, however, sometimes based on opinion only and may not necessarily be factual.

A trend which has been particularly welcomed by collectors is the publication of reproduction catalogues, details of which are given in the 'Further reading' section at the back of this book.

TRADEMARKS

In the latter part of the nineteenth century the practice of registering the design of goods was adopted in some countries, including Britain, where the Trademarks Registration Act was introduced in 1875, and registered numbers in 1884. Trademarks became an important aid to collectors in identifying the makers of toy steam engines and accessories.

A rare Meccano horizontal engine of about 1929, with vertical copper boiler, reversing lever and reduction gearing to driving pulley.

Some manufacturers, like Bing Brothers, used different marks for different periods and this is helpful in assessing the date of manufacture.

In addition to trademarks, a number of other markings were added from around 1890 to 1950. Some of the most common are:

Brevete SGDG: A French abbreviation for *Brevete sans Garantie du Gouvernement.*

DP ANG: a German patent mark meaning 'deposited'.

DRGM: a German abbreviation for *Deutsches Reich Gebrauch Muster*, a provisional patent mark meaning 'registered design'.

DRP: a German abbreviation for *Deutsches Reich Patent.*

England: a British patent marking (1891).

Gebrauchsmuster: a German mark for petty patents for improvements or alterations to toys already patented, or for which regular patents do not apply.

Ges Gesch, Ges G: a German copyright or patent mark covering designs which were 'by law protected'.

Made in England: a British patent marking (1900).

Made in Germany: a marking often used before 1939.

Made in US Zone Germany: an early post-Second World War German marking.

Made in Western Germany: a marking used since about 1948.

N: after a German trademark, this usually means made in Nuremberg.

Registered: a British patent marking (1884).

Unis France: means 'Union National Inter-Syndicate France'.

USP: United States patent.

CONCLUSION

The prototype steam engines, which have been reproduced in miniature as toys, were the most animated of man's inventions, breathing fire, belching smoke and hissing steam. Fortunately a wide variety of toy steam engines has survived, but most of them are owned by private collectors. Some of these collectors are now exhibiting their steam toys in museums, and one of the finest displays of this kind can be seen at the London Toy and Model Museum in Bayswater.

As well as being exciting to play with and fascinating to collect, steam toys are educational, and few toys provide such an excellent mixture of fun and education as those worked by steam, in which fire and water come together to produce mechanical energy.

Despite the many other attractions now available there is a continuing demand for steam engines, and chief among those keeping the tinplate steam toy business alive are three toymakers: the British firm of Mamod Limited, the American Jensen Manufacturing Company Incorporated, and the German Wilhelm Schroder and Company, makers of Wilesco steam toys.

ABOVE: *A selection of modern Mamod steam engines and accessories.*
BELOW, LEFT: *A modern Wilesco D45 vertical engine with mirror polished brass centre-flue boiler and firebox with embossed simulated brick walls, foot bridges with railings and ladder. The double-action cylinder is reversible, the boiler is heated with dry spirit tablets and the steam is exhausted up the chimney.*
BELOW, RIGHT: *A modern Jensen Number 10 horizontal double-acting power plant on a wooden base. The boiler is electrically-heated and the engine, which is fitted with a reversing lever, drives a 3.8 volt alternator.*

FURTHER READING

Greenly, Henry. *Model Steam Engines*. Percival Marshall, 1920s.
Hertz, Louis H. *The Handbook of Old American Toys*. Mark Haber, 1947.
McClintock, Marshall and Inez. *Toys In America*. Public Affairs Press, 1961.
Harley, Basil. *Toyshop Steam*. Model and Allied Publications, 1978.
Holland, G. William, Spong, Raymond, and Whitton, Blair. *American Live Steam Toys and Their Originators*. Antique Toy Collectors of America, 1978.
Kaiser, Wolf, and Baecker, J. Carlernst. *Battenberg Sammler-Kataloge: Blechspielzeug; Dampfspielzeug*. (Battenberg Collection Catalogue: Sheet Metal Toys; Steam Toys.) Battenberg Verlag, Munich, 1983.

REPRODUCTION CATALOGUES
Bassett-Lowke Railways (1902-63). Steam Age, 1969.
Gamages Christmas Bazaar (1913). David and Charles, 1974.
The Great Toys of Georges Carette (1911, and supplements for 1905-14). Allen Levy, New Cavendish Books, 1975.
Stevens's Model Dockyard (1919). TEE Publishing, 1978.
Mr Gamage's Great Toy Bazaar (1902-6). Denys Ingram, 1982.
Baecker, Carlernst, and Haas, Dieter. *Die Anderen Nürnberger* ('The Other Nurembergers'). Band 1 (1973): Karl Bub, Georges Carette and Company, John Distler KG, and Doll and Company. Band 2 (1973): J. Falk, Gebr Fleischmann, (SG) Gunthermann, Jos Kraus and Company, Ernst Paul Lehmann. Band 3 (1974): Johann And, Issmayer, George Levy, Ernst Plank, Tipp and Company. Band 4 (1975): Gebr Einfalt (Kosmos), Emil Hausmann, Jean Schoenner, Conrad Klein, A. Schuhmann. Band 5 (1976): Karl Arnold, Karl Bub, Moses Kohnstam, R and GN, Georges Carette, Schuco. Band 6 (1981): Ernst Paul Lehmann, Ullmann and Engelmann, Trix.

PLACES TO VISIT

Intending visitors are advised to find out the hours of opening before making a special journey.

British Engineerium, Nevill Road, Hove, East Sussex BN3 7QA. Telephone: Brighton (0273) 559583 or 554070.
Leeds Industrial Museum, Armley Mill, Canal Road, Armley, Leeds LS12 2QF. Telephone: Leeds (0532) 637861 or 637862.
London Toy and Model Museum, 23 Craven Hill, London W2. Telephone: 01-262 7905 or 9450.
Pollock's Toy Museum, 1 Scala Street, London W1P 1LT. Telephone: 01-636 3452.
Worthing Museum and Art Gallery, Chapel Road, Worthing, West Sussex BN11 1HQ. Telephone: Worthing (0903) 39999, extension 121. (Toy steam engines not always displayed.)